CLB 1757
© 1987 Colour Library Books Ltd, Guildford, Surrey, England
Printed and bound in Barcelona, Spain by Cronion, S.A.
ISBN 0 86283 556 9

THE
BRITISH ISLES

COLOUR LIBRARY BOOKS

LONDON

"Earth has not anything to show more fair:
Dull would he be of soul who could pass by
A sight so touching in its majesty:
·This City now doth like a garment wear

The beauty of the morning: silent, bare,
Ships, towers, domes, theatres, and temples lie
Open unto the fields, and to the sky,
All bright and glittering in the smokeless air."

Upon Westminster Bridge
(William Wordsworth)

Wordsworth's "mighty heart" of London is still there. Capital of Great Britain, it is a city which acts as the political, industrial and commercial centre of this majestic land, and was once the hub of the largest empire ever known. Its pre-eminence stems from its past: so many famous people have walked its streets; history weaves a rich tapestry through the ages and the story begins nearly two thousand years ago, back in Roman times...

Londinium was founded on the north side of the strategically important River Thames by the Roman invaders. However, they found that the fighting spirit of the native people was hard to crush: Boadicea, Queen of the Iceni – who occupied East Anglia – led an army which sacked the city. Eventually defeated in battle, she took her own life by poison in AD 62. Today, near the Houses of Parliament, a statue shows the warrior queen in her chariot with blades like scythes flashing from the wheel hubs. On the plinth beneath is enscribed the words, 'Regions Caesar never knew thy posterity shall sway'.

Take a walk nearer to the Palace of Westminster and there you will see the statue of a man who, throughout the darkest days of London, stood against the enemy's overwhelming forces; Sir Winston Churchill. Above him stands the clockface known as 'Big Ben', although it is really the 13½-ton bell within that was named after Sir Benjamin Hall and whose chimes are heard on BBC radio throughout the world. Nearby is Westminster Abbey, where the Kings and Queens of England have been crowned since William the Conqueror. It is also the burial place of the famous and includes Poet's Corner in the south transept, as well as the Tomb of the Unknown Soldier.

In Whitehall you come to the Cenotaph, memorial to the dead of both World Wars. Further on the left is Downing Street, the home of the Prime Minister, and you will see Horse Guards as well before you arrive at Trafalgar Square. This is dominated by Nelson's Column and Landseer's lions, and the National Gallery with its wide selection of the world's great masters: the vibrant sunflowers and corn fields of Van Gogh; the elaborate garden of Monet; the English countryside of Constable; the Venetian waterways of Canaletto; the coloured light of Turner and many other favourites.

Perhaps by now you will be feeling exhausted. But walk just a little way up Charing Cross Road and turn left into Soho. Here you can find a cosy wine bar or coffee shop in which to recuperate. Now the evening's entertainment may begin. The narrow, bustling streets throng with people and bright lights shine. Restaurants, theatres, night clubs and cinemas abound in this most cosmopolitan of areas. Tomorrow there will be time for more of London's attractions: St Paul's Cathedral designed by Sir Christopher Wren; Buckingham Palace, home of the Royal Family; shopping in Oxford Street or at Harrods; Speakers' Corner in Hyde Park where anyone can stand on a soapbox to speak their mind; a visit to the Tower of London, or perhaps to see one of the many museums.

This colourful book brings refreshing views of the capital city, with vivid photographs showing the vitality and variety of life in London. As Samuel Johnson wrote, "When a man is tired of London he is tired of life; for there is in London all that life can afford".

Opposite page: (top left) gazing resolutely across Parliament Square stands the statue of Sir Winston Churchill by Ivor Roberts-Jones. (Bottom left) Nelson's Column, Trafalgar Square. At the base of the column are four bronze reliefs, cast from captured French cannons, which show scenes from the naval battles which made Nelson a national hero: St Vincent, Copenhagen, The Nile and Trafalgar. (Right) Trafalgar Square and its spouting fountains. This page: (below) Landseer's lions, which surround the foot of the column, were cast from cannon recovered from the wreck of the *Royal George* which sank at Spithead in 1782. (Left) the Houses of Parliament and Westminster Bridge seen at night.

Opposite page: (top left) St Paul's Cathedral and *HMS Discovery*, taken to the Antarctic in 1900 by Captain Scott. (Top right) the White Tower of the Tower of London. (Centre left) Lambeth Bridge and the Houses of Parliament. (Centre right) Richmond Bridge. (Bottom left) Tower Bridge. (Bottom right) view from the National Westminster Tower. This page: (left and below) the Thames. (Bottom) St Katherine's Dock and Tower Hotel.

9

These pages: on special ceremonial occasions, such as Trooping the Colour, the regiments of Guards may be seen resplendent in their scarlet and black uniforms. The metal and leather accoutrements of the soldiers gleam as they march and ride in proud precision. They protect the London home of the Queen – Buckingham Palace (above) – where the ceremony of Changing the Guard may be seen daily. The knowledgeable can differentiate between Grenadier, Coldstream, Scots, Irish and Welsh Guards by the different spacing of their brass tunic buttons. Opposite page: (centre left) Queen Elizabeth II takes the salute of her soldiers.

Opposite page: the dome and cross of St Paul's Cathedral rise high above the gilded River Thames, dominating the buildings around. This page: (top left) Tower Bridge looms out of the grey mist. (Top right) the setting sun stains a golden path across the river as it wends its way through the heart of the city. (Above) illuminated Chelsea Bridge. Up river from London's centre, near Kew, is the hamlet of Strand-on-the-Green (far left). Richmond-upon-Thames (centre left and left) is the site of an old royal palace.

13

This page: (top) the White Tower is the oldest part of the Tower of London, dating from about 1078. (Right) wardens of the Tower of London. Opposite page: (top left) the Law Courts in the Strand. (Top right) known as The Monument, this pillar was built in 1672-1677 to commemorate the Great Fire of London of 1666, which devastated two-thirds of the capital in the course of five days. (Bottom left) part of the old Roman city wall, built at the end of the second century AD. (Bottom right) St Paul's Cathedral viewed from Cardinal Cap Alley, across the River Thames.

This page: (top left) Buckingham Palace. (Centre left) the Royal Festival Hall. (Top right) the Royal Albert Hall. (Above and right) Westminster Abbey. Opposite page: traffic in Whitehall. The light which burns in the Clock Tower shows that Parliament is sitting. By day, a Union Jack flying above the Victoria Tower of the Palace of Westminster – usually called the Houses of Parliament – demonstrates the same.

This page: (above) the Thames, coloured a delicate shade of mauve. (Top right) the Bank of England and Royal Exchange. (Centre right) each day, the population of London increases dramatically as commuters arrive for work by car, train and tube.

(Right) the National Westminster Tower is the tallest building in London and is 600 feet high with 52 floors. (Below) Fleet Street, famous as the 'Street of Ink'. Opposite page: Paddington Station, which provides train services to the west.

Opposite page: the aerial photograph demonstrates that London contains many areas of restful parks and greens. St James's Park and Green Park can be seen set amid the grand buildings of Whitehall and The Mall, at the end of which is Buckingham Palace. Red buses scurry around Parliament Square and the panorama stretches out to the far horizon. This page: (top left) Regent's Park Canal. (Far left and left) riding or resting, Hyde Park is a lovely place to visit. (Above) within Kew Gardens, world famous for its collection of plants and trees, and its scientific research. (Top right) Old Deer Park, Richmond, scene of the last known duel in England.

This page: some of the wonderful pubs of London. As Samuel Johnson said, 'There is nothing which has been contrived by man by which so much happiness is produced as by a good tavern or inn'. (Above) the Old Bull and Bush between Hampstead and Golders Green. (Right) outside Solange's wine bar after a wedding. (Bottom right) the Wheatsheaf. (Below) The Flask, in Highgate, was frquented long ago by Dick Turpin, the infamous highwayman, and later, by William Hogarth, the engraver and painter. Opposite page: Regent's Park Canal.

This page: (top left) the neon lights of Piccadilly Circus. (Centre left) Lambeth Bridge and the Houses of Parliament (top right). (Above) the Post Office Tower. (Right) the Royal Festival Hall. Opposite page: (top) Hampton Court Palace, built by Cardinal Wolsey in 1515. (Bottom) the riverside on the South Bank.

This page: examples of the many scenes that London conjures to the mind. (Above) the 'clippie' on the bus. (Right) cricket on the green. (Below) open-air fruit market. (Centre right) bewigged barristers. (Bottom right) a Yeoman Warder.

This page: (left) a military band plays at the bandstand in Hyde Park. (Bottom left) mews cottages in Hampstead. (Below) the statue of Peter Pan – the boy who never grew up – in Kensington Gardens. (Bottom right) the intricate design on the Albert Memorial.

Previous page: the Albert Memorial, erected in memory of the Prince Consort. Top left: members of the Society of Toastmasters raise their glasses to the newly-married Prince and Princess of Wales. Centre left and above: London 'bobbies' on the beat. Left: pensioners of the Royal Hospital, Chelsea. Facing page: the magnificent Hampton Court Palace, presented to Henry VIII in 1526, remained a royal residence until the time of George III.

These pages: in the light of dawn or dusk, reflected from the waters of the Thames or seen through the enveloping mists of morning, London is a city of grandeur, its very stones echoing the remorseless passage of time. Opposite page: (top left) a silhouetted bronze griffin marks Temple Bar and the City boundary. It replaced a gate upon which, until 1745, the heads of executed villains were set as an example to any who might have cared to follow the path of the criminal.

This page: (right) Tower Bridge.
(Above, below and opposite page:
top) St Paul's Cathedral.
(Bottom left) the statue of
Boadicea near the Clock Tower.
(Centre left) 'Justice' above
the Old Bailey. (Centre right)
choristers in the Tower of
London. (Bottom right) Trafalgar
Square's Christmas tree is
presented each year by Norway.

Opposite page: (top) the Queen's House, Greenwich – in the centre of the picture – was built for Anne of Denmark and, upon her death, for the wife of Charles I; Henrietta Maria. The colonnades link it to the National Maritime Museum. (Bottom) Buckingham Palace and St James's Park, through which Charles I walked, from St James's Palace to Horse Guards, on his way to the block. This page: (far left) the Pagoda in Kew Gardens. (Left) Richmond-upon-Thames. (Below) schoolgirls near Sloane Street. (Bottom) Kenwood House, Hampstead.

This page: (below and right) the Bank of England, on the left, and the beautiful facade of the Royal Exchange. (Bottom) the crypt chapel of St Stephen's in the Palace of Westminster. Opposite page: (top left) the clipper *Cutty Sark* in dry dock at Greenwich. (Remaining pictures) St Paul's Cathedral.

This page: (right) a Guard stands lonely vigil. (Bottom and far right) the Houses of Parliament and the Clock Tower. The statue is of Jan Christiaan Smuts. Opposite page: (top) the Queen Victoria Memorial, outside Buckingham Palace, with The Mall leading away to Admiralty Arch. (Top right) Horse Guards in Whitehall. (Bottom left) the Royal Staircase in the Houses of Parliament and (bottom right) the Robing Room. The painting shows Christ and Sir Galahad, the knight who could sit in the Siege Perilous of King Arthur's Round Table without risk of his life and who succeeded in the quest of the Holy Grail.

ENGLAND

England is a magical kingdom where mystery and history blend with the prosaic and the present to create a realm which is unique. Whether the scene is a ruined castle or a bustling city street, a windswept moor or a lush, green meadow, it has been permeated for centuries with the charm, serenity and excitement that make it peculiarly English. The land has an atmosphere which can be mistaken for that of nowhere else on earth.

It has long been said that the salt water of the sea courses through the veins of every true Englishman. For centuries the men of this island nation have ploughed the seven seas in search of trade or plunder. The spray-drenched rocks of Land's End, with screaming sea birds circling above them, have been the last sight many a man has had of his native land. It is only fitting, therefore, that a ghostly galleon can sometimes be seen bringing its phantom crew back to those same sea-smashed cliffs to which its living crew never returned.

But not all the shores of England are as inhospitable as the towering cliffs of Cornwall. Many miles of the sparkling coastline are ringed with golden sands which attract holidaymakers in their thousands. When the warm summer sun glitters on the shifting sea and a cooling breeze brushes the sands, there can be no better place than an English beach.

Beyond the horizon where sea meets land stretch the rich fields that have made England wealthy. Winding, tree-shaded lanes snake for miles across the fertile lowlands. Along these hedgerowed byways, which now resound to the clatter of the motorcar, strode generations of farmers and shepherds. No matter how far the road may wind, nor through what scenery it may weave its course, it will have a town as its destination.

Every town in England has its individual character and is like no other, yet they are all uncompromisingly English. The bustling capital city of London lies in the Thames Basin glowing with history and pulsating with life. It was here that William the Conqueror was crowned King of England. Through these streets the crowds cheered Nelson after each new victory. But if there is a city which looks to the future, that city is London. Shiny, new office blocks climb hundreds of feet into the sky, symbols of future prosperity, just as the historical monuments signify a wealthy past.

Further north, the academic town of Cambridge raises its beautiful architecture above the rich farmland. For nearly eight centuries students have come here to stroll the cloistered pathways and to learn. Beautiful King's College Chapel is acknowledged to be the finest example of Perpendicular Gothic in the world. Yet this is only one building amongst many. Cambridge is rich with churches, chapels, gatehouses and quadrangles, any one of which is magnificent in its own right.

The ancient capital of Northumbria, York, stands proudly on the Ouse. Its beautiful Minster is the very heart of the North. Surrounding the great city rise the windswept moors where even the hardy sheep must find shelter from the howling gale. At times the dank, impenetrable fog will lower itself onto the desolate hills and make the tors drip with dampness. It seems as if the land weeps for the lost soul of Eric Bloodaxe, last independent King of York, who was slain by a traitor at 'a certain lonely place which is called Stainmore'.

Across the face of England, in every county and on every coast, can be found the ruined relics of medieval splendour. The castles of the rich and powerful once echoed to the clank of armour, the fluttering of banners and the laughter of men and women. Now they stand roofless and silent.

The elegant arches of the monasteries, rising above the green fields, are no less silent and deserted. Gentle breezes waft the grass and scatter the dry leaves through the splintered cloisters, while the walls seem to echo the peaceful chants of the holy men of long ago. That same breeze can gather in force and speed until it whips the leaves across the land. Dark clouds can gather to blot out the moon, and lightning may streak across the skies. The rushing wind can shake the trees so that they twist and buck dementedly. On such furious nights the booming thunder may be taken for drumming hooves and in the howling wind can be heard the laughter of the Devil as he urges the Wild Hunt across the tumultuous skies.

England is a country with many faces, warm and welcoming or proud and defiant. The eye can never tire of its beauty, nor the senses of its atmosphere. It is truly a magical land.

Previous page: beautiful, medieval Wells Cathedral, Somerset. Perhaps the most secure natural harbour for small craft on the north coast of Cornwall is Boscastle (left). Its narrow, winding entrance and towering cliffs provide almost perfect protection from the ocean waves. In contrast, the jagged rocks of Cornwall's Land's End (below), marked by Longships Lighthouse, are open to the wild seas. Bottom: the curious formation of Bedruthan's Steps, north of Newquay in Cornwall.

Below: Inner Harbour at Falmouth, the busiest port in Cornwall (these pages). Smaller, but with their own particular charm, are the Cornish ports of Polperro (below centre), and Cadgwith (bottom). St Mawes (right) takes its name from a Celtic monk who for many years lived as a hermit beside a well renowned for the curative properties of its waters.

44

Newquay (above and left), in Cornwall (these pages), was named after a quay built in the 16th century for the fishing town of Towan Blystra. Penzance harbour (top) shelters one of the lightships which lie anchored off the coast to warn ships of treacherous waters.

Below: small boats beached at low tide in the popular resort of St Ives, in Cornwall (these pages). Bottom: Longships Lighthouse off Land's End. Scattered across the face of the county are several castles and strongholds, of which the ruins of Launceston Castle (right) are an outstanding example. Far right: the remains of Tintagel Castle, built in 1145 for Reginald, the then Earl of Cornwall and illegitimate son of Henry I. It was abandoned during the 15th century and has been left to decline ever since.

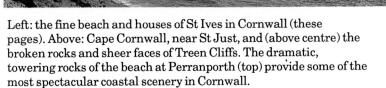

Left: the fine beach and houses of St Ives in Cornwall (these pages). Above: Cape Cornwall, near St Just, and (above centre) the broken rocks and sheer faces of Treen Cliffs. The dramatic, towering rocks of the beach at Perranporth (top) provide some of the most spectacular coastal scenery in Cornwall.

51

These pages: the county of Cornwall. Above left: a fisherman displaying his catch in Cadgwith, and (above right) the coastal village of Polperro. Top: Longships Lighthouse seen from the air, and (right) the rugged, fractured cliffs around Land's End.

When the tide runs out many of Cornwall's drowned river valleys, or rias, are exposed as broad mudflats cut by small streams, like the Looe Estuary (right), where small boats lie stranded on the mudflats. Below: sunset over Cape Cornwall's coast just north of Land's End, and (bottom) St Michael's Mount at sunrise, Cornwall.

Above: the whitewashed houses of Polperro in Cornwall (these pages), and (left) Mevagissey, a bustling village where small shops and brightly-painted fishing craft crowd the harbour below the cottages. Top: St Michael's Mount at low tide, when the stone causeway stands revealed above the water.

Salcombe (above), with its wooded hills and boat-filled harbour, is one of the most beautifully-situated towns in Devon (these pages). Top: thatched roofs in Cockington, one of the county's lovely villages. Right: the River Exe flows past a pub at Bickleigh.

58

Bottom: the granite church of St Pancras at Widecombe-in-the-Moor, with its 135-foot-high, 16th-century tower, on Dartmoor in Devon. Bottom right: a thatched cottage at Bucks Mills, and (remaining pictures) the tourist showplace of Clovelly, Devon.

Torquay (left) is the largest and best-served resort in Devon (these pages). Above right: elegant, 1526 fan vaulting seen in the Lane Aisle of Cullompton Church, and (above left) the pulpit of Ashprington Church. Top: the spectacular red cliffs and gentle farmland which surround Sidmouth.

Four centuries ago, Ilfracombe (left), in Devon (these pages), was an important port. Today tourism makes it the largest resort on the north coast. Below left: the village of Clovelly. Below centre: Jacob's Ladder at Sidmouth, and (bottom) the wild crags of the Valley of the Rocks near Lynton which inspired Shelley.

When William the Conqueror finally captured Exeter two years after the Battle of Hastings, he imposed his authority on Devon (these pages). One of the most solid signs of the changing times came when the Saxon cathedral at Exeter was demolished and a Norman edifice built in its place. In turn, most of the Norman church has been replaced by the splendid Gothic cathedral (right) seen today. The church of Bridford (above) lies near Dartmoor, and boasts a splendid rood screen made in 1508. The 14th-century church of St Peter (top), in Cornworthy, has a fine Georgian exterior.

Facing page: the mile-long beach at Seaton, near the mouth of the Yarty. Above left: Clovelly, and (above right) Bowerman's Nose on Dartmoor in Devon (these pages). Top: Buckland-in-the-Moor, and (left and above left) Widecombe-in-the-Moor, Dartmoor. Top left: the isolated church of Brentnor.

69

Above: Sir Walter Raleigh's birthplace in Hayes Barton. Combe
Martin (top), as its name might suggest, lies in a combe reaching
down to the sea, and has a small beach of both pebbles and sand.
Above centre: Hoops Inn. Right: the sandy stretches of Exmouth
beach seen from Orcombe Point.

Dartington Hall (bottom) was built in the closing years of the 14th century by John Holland, half-brother to King Richard II, and is one of the finest secular mediaeval buildings in the southwest of Devon (these pages). On the highest hill in Dartmouth stands the Royal Naval College (below), which was completed in 1905 to the plans of Sir Aston Webb. Right: a full scale replica of the Elizabethan warship the *Golden Hind* and a monument to William III on the quayside at Brixham.

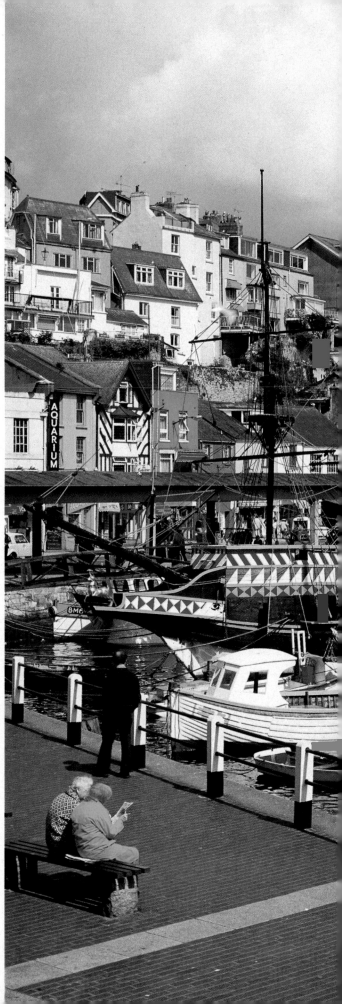

72

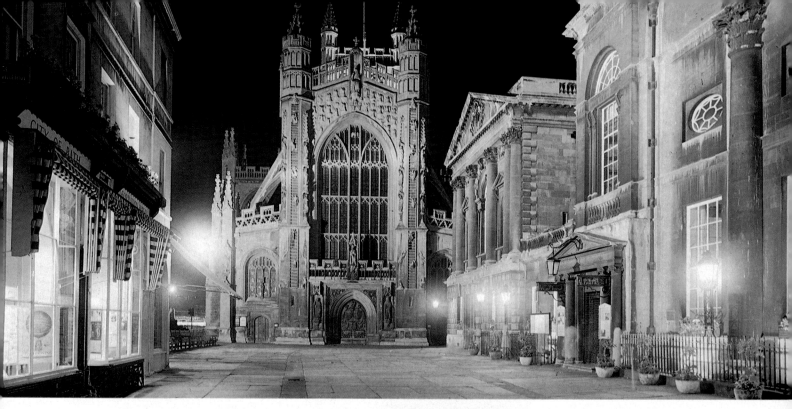

Facing page: (top and bottom left) splendid Bath Abbey, Avon, and (bottom right) magnificent Cheddar Gorge, Somerset. Avon's fine bridges include (above) Bath's shop-lined Pulteney Bridge, (far left and top) the imposing Clifton Suspension Bridge and (left and overleaf) the Severn Suspension Bridge. Above left: the solid packhorse bridge at Allerford in Somerset.

Above: the west front of Wells
Cathedral (top and left) in Somerset
(remaining pictures), originally
embellished with nearly 400 statues of
saints, angels and prophets. Top left
and right: the ruins of Glastonbury's
13th-century abbey, Somerset. It was
here that Joseph of Arimathea came to
convert the English. As he leant on his
staff to pray, it reputably took root,
indicating that the saint should found a
religious house here. Overleaf: (left)
Bibury village, and (right) the mill at
Lower Slaughter, both in the Cotswolds,
Gloustershire.

A sense of timelessness sets the Gloucestershire region of the Cotswolds (these pages and overleaf) apart from any other. Right: beautiful Tewkesbury Abbey, and (below) fine Gloucester Cathedral. Below right: Dursley, (facing page bottom) Naunton, (facing page top) Chipping Campden and (overleaf) Upper Slaughter, all villages built of mellow local stone. Above: St John's Lock at Lechlade.

Previous pages: (left) Worcester Cathedral, mainly of the Early-English to Perpendicular period and (right) St Andrew's Church, noted for its superb, early-14th-century lantern tower, both in Hereford and Worcester. Right: an old water-mill completes a setting of black and white half-timbered buildings at Tewkesbury in Gloucestershire. The soaring Gothic spire of St Mary the Virgin dominates the evening sky of the marcher town of Ross-on-Wye in Hereford and Worcester (remaining pictures), and the church of All Saints (above) is one of two notable churches in the elegant market town of Evesham. Above right: the thatched roof of Holland House in Cropthorne. Facing page: spring brings daffodils to the old churchyard in Upton Bishop (top) and freshens the rolling countryside (bottom).

Facing page: the Wye meanders through farmland below Symond's Yat in Hereford and Worcester (these pages). This is a beautiful county in which timber-framed cottages (this page) lend an air of old-worldliness to their surroundings, as does Church Lane to the lovely town of Ledbury (below). Overleaf: (left) the magnificent cathedral at Salisbury, and (right) Longleat House, Wiltshire.

Built in the dawn of history, Stonehenge (this page) was a pagan construction whose fame extended even as far as ancient Crete. The mystery as to its exact purpose continues to fascinate archeologists, as does the Avebury Stone Circle (facing page top left). Facing page: (top right) the dining room of the Renaissance house of Longleat, and (bottom) stone cottages in Castle Combe, Wiltshire (these pages). Overleaf: (left) the 14th-century tithe barn in Bradford-on-Avon, and (right) Stourhead, Wiltshire.

Near Lulworth in Dorset (these pages) lies some spectacular coastal scenery including Durdle Door (above, facing page bottom and overleaf right), a huge limestone arch which juts out into the sea at Man o' War Bay (overleaf left). Above left: a church in Affpuddle, a typical Thomas Hardy town. Below: Corfe Castle, dominated by its castle ruins. Left: Boscombe, and (facing page top) Weymouth, both popular resorts.

Rolling Devon farmland at Harcombe (facing page) is typical of southern England's landscape. Cerne Abbas (above left) nestles in the Dorset countryside and is named after a Benedictine abbey founded there in 987. Left: Corfe Castle, and (above) the huge 'Osmington Man', both in Dorset.

Above: a beautifully-manicured thatched roof, (right) equally well-kept Quay Hill in Lymington and (below) an ocean liner in Southampton, Hampshire. Facing page: (top) horses grazing in the village of Bucklers Hard, (centre) canoes and a ferry boat in Portsmouth and (bottom) the river at Lymington, all in Hampshire. Overleaf: Yarmouth, on the Isle of Wight, Hampshire.

Above: mighty Arundel Castle, seen across the Arun River, (above right) seafront gardens at Eastbourne and (right) water-lilies on one of the five lakes in Sheffield Park Gardens, Sussex. Facing page: (top) Shoreham-by-Sea, (bottom left) the resort of Eastbourne, (bottom right) Birling Gap and (overleaf) Bosham harbour, Sussex.

113

Previous pages: (left) the 600-foot-high chalk cliffs of Beachy Head in Sussex, and (right) the Pantiles at Royal Tunbridge Wells in Kent (these pages). Facing page: (top) Scotney Castle, and (bottom) Leeds Castle. Left: Farmingham and (above) Aylesford, two of the county's villages that time seems to have passed by. Below: an oast house.

Previous pages: Canterbury Cathedral, Kent. Above:
Guildford's Guildhall, (above right) Chiddingfold, and
(right) Wentworth Golf Club, Surrey (these pages and
overleaf). Facing page: (top) idyllic landscapes and
(bottom) an old cottage near Lingfield. Overleaf: (left)
Broadwater Lake, Godalming, and (right) the massive
Norman keep, nearly all that remains of Guildford Castle.

Right: sunlight filters through trees, and (facing page) veils of mist trail among fields and woodland in Surrey (these pages). Overleaf: (right) Windsor in Berkshire, where Windsor Castle (left) overlooks the Thames, having guarded the western approaches to London since William the Conqueror's time.

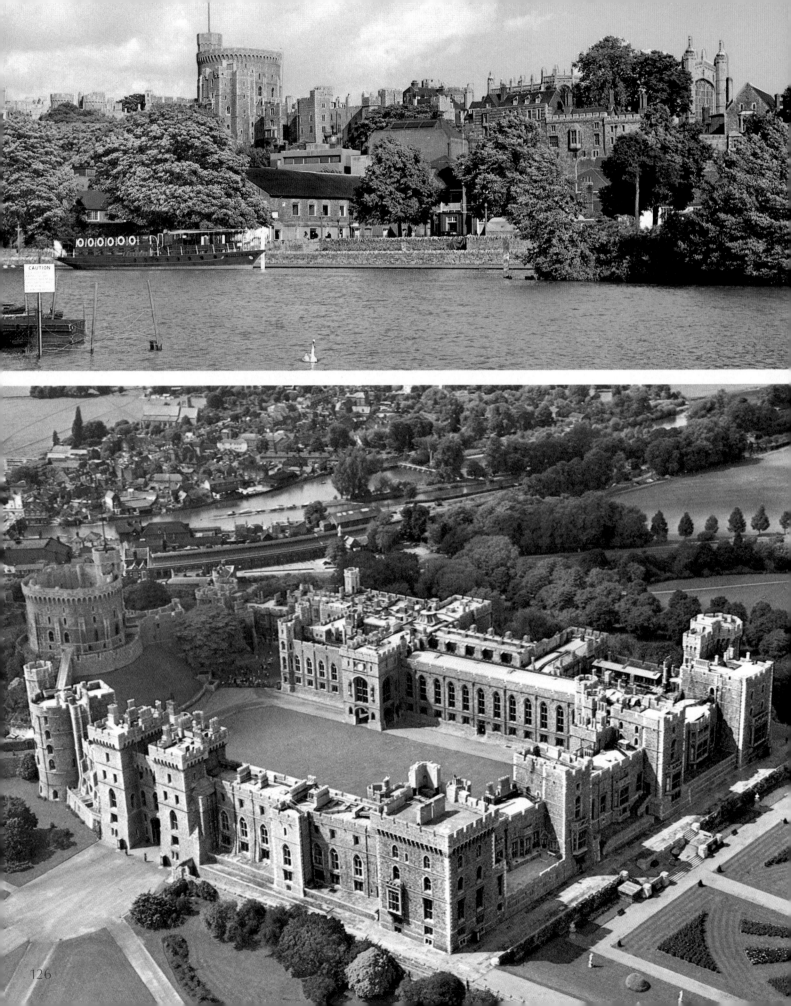

Of England's palaces, none can surely be more stately or famous than the Queen's home in Berkshire - Windsor Castle (facing page). Not far from London, it is within easy reach of visitors to the capital. Apart from its castle, Windsor itself is well worth seeing, and Church Street (top) is one of its loveliest areas. Above left: Priors Croft, at Dorney in Berkshire. Overleaf: Merton College, founded in 1264 and seen from Christchurch Meadows.

A cricket match (right) is very much part of the English summer scene, as is a lock full of small boats such as at Wallingford (bottom) in Oxfordshire. It was in the same county, at Henley (bottom right), in 1839, that the world's first river regatta was held, a tradition that still continues each year, attracting many competitors and spectators. Below: a tranquil summer's day at Whitchurch in Buckinghamshire. Facing page: the Oxford college of Christ Church, founded by Cardinal Wolsey in 1525. Overleaf: Blenheim Palace in Oxfordshire.

Previous pages: (left) the partly-Norman church at Medmenham, and (right) the Hambledon Mill, both in Buckinghamshire. Right: Epping Forest, (above) Finchingfield and (top) Clacton-on-Sea, all in Essex. Facing page: (top left) Kersey, (top right) Cavendish and (bottom) Lavenham, all villages in Suffolk.

141

Previous pages: King's College Chapel, Cambridge University. Queens' College (left), Cambridge, was founded no less than three times in the course of the 15th century, while Trinity Hall (bottom), also part of Cambridge University, was founded in 1350 by the Bishop of Norwich. Below: the lovely bridge of Trinity College over the River Cam, and (facing page) the "Bridge of Sighs", which links two of the buildings of St John's College, Cambridge. Bottom left: King's College Chapel, Cambridge. Ely Cathedral (below left), Cambridgeshire, was begun in 1083 and is a magnificent sight even from a distance.

The American Cemetery (this page), in
Cambridgeshire, honours the memory of
servicemen who lost their lives in combat
during World War II. Above: the interior of
the cemetery's Memorial. Facing page: (top)
Christ's College, and (bottom) Neville's Court,
Trinity College, Cambridge.

The Classical mansion of
Chatsworth House (above) stands in
the midst of gentle countryside in
Derbyshire (these pages). Top:
pleasure boats lie at their moorings
in Whaley Bridge, while (right) the
River Lathkill tumbles over a
waterfall. Facing page: (top)
Castleton, a fine town at the western
entrance to the Hope Valley, and
(bottom) the Roaches seen from Hen
Clouds, near Leek.

These pages and overleaf:
Stratford-upon-Avon in
Warwickshire. Top and above
left: the Royal Shakespeare
Theatre, by the Avon (below).
Facing page top: Shakespeare's
birthplace, (left and overleaf left)
Holy Trinity church, his burial
place, and (remaining pictures)
Anne Hathaway's cottage, the
family home of his wife.

Despite industrialisation, Warwickshire (these pages) still has leafy lanes as well as fine towns such as Warwick, containing lovely Bridge End (above). Wootton Hall (right) is a beautiful, 17th-century house at Wootton Wawen, and the manor house of Compton Wynyates (facing page) is a superb example of Tudor architecture, with its stone and brick offset by yews and hedges tailored into neat, formal shapes. Top: Welford-on-Avon.

Above and top: Eastgate Street and (facing page) Chester Cathedral in Chester (overleaf left), and (left) Little Moreton Hall, Cheshire. Overleaf right: the Playhouse, Liverpool.

Facing page: (top) Liverpool Docks, and (bottom and below) the famed Liver Building, Liverpool (these pages). Bottom: the modern interior of the Roman Catholic Metropolitan Cathedral, and (bottom left) the Anglican Cathedral. Left: Sefton Park, which provides a welcome retreat for city dwellers. Overleaf: (left) cobbled Steep Hill in Lincoln, and (right) Blackpool, dominated by its 520-foot-tall tower.

Blackpool's famous promenade (facing page) runs beside sandy beaches for over six miles, overlooked by its tower which contains a ballroom (top), while its "Golden Mile" beach (above) is packed with funfair attractions. Left: Manchester's Perpendicular Gothic Cathedral.

165

Above: the fine civic hall in Leeds, W. Yorkshire, and (right) the River Nidd at Knaresborough in N. Yorkshire (remaining pictures). York is famous for its old city walls (above right), built on Roman foundations, which gird the city for 3 miles. Whitby (left and top) is dominated by the jagged sandstone ruins of its abbey, while Scarborough (overleaf) is overlooked by 12th-century castle ruins. Top right: red-roofed cottages in Robin Hood's Bay.

Facing page top: the Minster, (top) St Mary's Abbey , and (above) the Shambles, York, N. Yorkshire. Facing page: (bottom left) a 'Druids Temple', (bottom right) walls near Malham, and (left) Westondale, Yorkshire Dales. Overleaf: (left) Whitby harbour, N. Yorkshire. (Right) Tyne Bridge and the Swing Bridge, Newcastle-Upon-Tyne, Tyne and Wear.

Below: the 16th-century castle of Lindisfarne on Holy Island, off the Northumbrian coast, (right) wildflowers in the Yorkshire Dales and (bottom) Durham Cathedral, Co. Durham. Facing page: Roman Hadrian's Wall, built from the Tyne to the Solway. Overleaf: (left) Ullswater, and (right) Watendlath, in the Lake District.

Left: the silky, rushing waters of High Force, a waterfall in Gowbarrow Park above Ullswater, in the Lake District (these pages and overleaf), Cumbria. Above: the blue waters of Buttermere, a one-and-a-quarter-mile-long lake near the village of the same name.
Top: a rugged stone bridge across a beck above Derwent Water, and (overleaf) Ennerdale Water.

These pages and overleaf: the Lake District, Cumbria. Left: the small, 12th-century church at Grasmere, the burial place of William Wordsworth. The curious, squat pinnacles of its tower are echoed in a church at Troutbeck (top), which stands in a valley off Windermere. The spired church of Keswick (above) was founded by St Kentigern after he had fled from the pagan King Morken of Strathclyde. Overleaf: sunset over Derwent Water, usually the first lake to freeze over in winter, due to its shallowness.

These pages and overleaf: the Lake District. Left: the Kirkstile Inn and its accompanying church nestled beneath towering crags, making it one of the most spectacularly-sited pubs in the kingdom. Top: sun-drenched fields and moorland at Roughton, north of Ennerdale Water. A shepherd (above) drives his flock along a country lane, between traditional dry-stone walls, in the beautiful valley of Longsleddale.

Left: the cold light of dawn creeps through the mist and casts long shadows across the banks of Ullswater in the Lake District (these pages and overleaf), Cumbria. This scenic stretch of water has lost little of its charm in recent years, though it lost its centuries-old importance as a county boundary when Cumberland and Westmorland disappeared beneath bureaucratic reorganisation. Top: a band of low cloud passes across the craggy face of the Langdale Pikes, and (above) the steep, eroded slopes of Derwent Fells rise above the narrow Keskadale Pass. Overleaf: the principle of the arch is rarely seen to better effect than in this ancient bridge across the Wasdale Beck.

Top: the tiny Cumbrian hamlet of Watendlath in the Lake District (these pages), which lies along the hanging valley of the same name. Its small, stone-built settlement is reached by a steep road and is so remote that it only recently gained electricity Above: Crummock Water, a two-and-a-half-mile-long lake, fed from Buttermere to the south. Right: snow covers the slopes above Tom's Howe farm in Longsleddale beside the River Sprint.

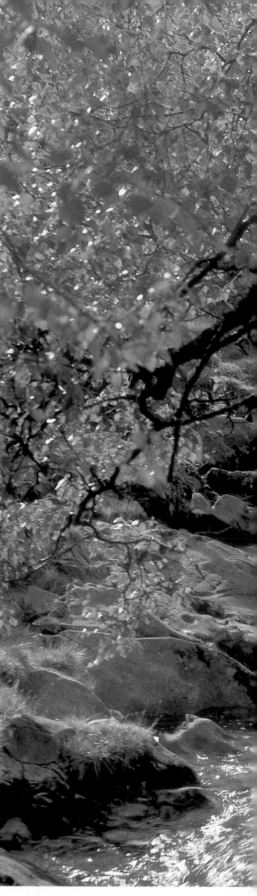

These pages: the Lake District in
Cumbria. Left: the tree-lined shores
of Grasmere, declared by
Wordsworth to be ' the loveliest spot
that man hath ever found'. Top left:
sheep-grazed slopes in the lower

hills. Above: near Ambleside, the
tumbling waters of the beck of
Scandale pass beneath a narrow
and ancient stone bridge of a
pattern often found in this region.

These pages and overleaf: the Lake District. Left: Yewtree Farm near Coniston, a typical Cumbrian farm. The whitewashed stone farmhouse, with its slate roof, is a fine example of the type of building which proliferated after 1640 when increasing prosperity made farmers rich enough to rebuild their wooden houses in stone. Earlier structures would have had more in common with Yewtree Farm's half-timbered outbuildings. The dry-stone walls which surround the farm, and which occur again at Wasdale (top) are generally less than two centuries old. It was only after 1750 that it paid farmers to graze and improve the fellsides, and the picturesque dry-stone walls are a mark of their endeavours. Above: the rising heights of Crinkle Craggs and Bow Fell from the slopes of Pike of Blisco. Overleaf: Ullswater.

Above: a sweeping view of Derwent Water from Lodore Wood in the Lake District of Cumbria (these pages and overleaf). Top: a beckside road winds towards the snow-capped summit of Langdale Pikes. Right: a view from Borrowdale, across Derwent Water to the peaks of Skiddaw and Little Man. Overleaf: the wintery stretches of Haweswater, magnificently set at the foot of the great scooped valley of Riggindale Beck, seen from Marsdale Banks.

These pages: the Lake District in Cumbria. Above: Gatesgarth and the southern end of Buttermere, with the peaks of Haystacks, Great Gable, High Crag and Scafell Pike, among others, reaching to the winter horizon. Top right: a view of Grasmere from Red Bank. Right: the mysterious megalithic circle of Castlerigg, where ten stones stand in a rectangle surrounded by a circle of 38 more. The stones have

stood here for millennia, since the
first men came to the Lake District.

Above: horses, once the most viable form of transport in the fells, graze quietly beneath the towering peaks of the Lake District (these pages), Cumbria. Top: the snow-covered peaks of Crinkle Crags to the left, and Bow Fell to the right, as seen from beside the small stone bridge across Great Langdale Beck. Above the wild, windswept valley where the Romans built their fort of Mediobogdum rises the rocky crag of Border End, which provides fine views north to Scafell Pike (right). Border End can only be reached from the exceptionally steep and twisted Hard Knott Pass.

WALES

The Principality of Wales juts from the west coast of England, separated from the West Country to the south by the Bristol Channel, and with the Isle of Man and, eventually, the Scottish Lowlands to the north.

Linking the Brecon Beacons and Black Mountains in the south with the Snowdonia and Clwydian ranges in the north, the Cambrian Mountains form the backbone of Wales. Here, in the south-east of the principality, the Snowdon Range and the mountains of Merioneth form the highest peaks in Britain south of the Scottish border. Indeed, some of the most impressive scenery in the whole of the British Isles is to be found in Wales: magnificent mountains, cascading waterfalls, winding streams, remote lakes and hills, heather-clad moors and a wild and glorious coastline encompassing rocky shores and broad, sandy beaches.

Wales was always, and remains, a country to stir the imagination; a country of myth and folklore, poetry and song; all products of the mystic quality of the landscape. It comes as no surprise, therefore, to find that South Wales, for instance, is particularly rich in its associations with the fabulous tales of King Arthur and his Knights of the Round Table. One of the central figures in the stories, Merlin, the legendary wizard, is said to have been born in Carmarthen, in the south-east, and it is believed that he cast a spell on an oak tree in Priory Street, declaring that, should the tree ever fall, so would the town. Fanciful? Perhaps. But the rotting stump can be seen even today, supported by iron bands and embedded in concrete! Such is the strength of legend.

Not far from Carmarthen is the picturesque harbour and old town of Laugharne, the home for many years of Dylan Thomas and the model, so it is said, for his now classic radio drama *Under Milk Wood*.

Wales abounds in the unexpected. Here is the smallest house in Britain, and here, too, the longest place-name, virtually unpronounceable to all but the Welsh. The village of Portmerion, inspired by the Italian village of Portofino, and the realisation of a dream by the architect Clough Williams-Ellis, finds itself perfectly at home in its Welsh coastal setting. Here is the Tal-y-Llyn Railway, the oldest steam-hauled, narrow gauge railway in the world; St David's, Britain's smallest cathedral city, and Mynydd Prescelly, where the blocks for the building of Stonehenge were quarried. And so it goes on, always the unexpected, the unusual, and always the mystic, brooding quality of the landscape.

Despite the extensive coal and iron mining that once provided so much employment – albeit with its attendant tragedies and heartaches – for the people of the valleys of Wales, much of the landscape remains unspoilt. Indeed, the clearing of tips and planting of trees around now-disused mines is bringing about the recovery of even this once scarred landscape.

The shores of Wales provide sanctuary for great colonies of seabirds and seals, and inland there are red squirrels, otters, pine marten, deer and wild ponies. There are even herds of white cattle in the north that are said to be descended from Roman cows. The moorlands support a variety of plant life and in the south-west there are exotic flowers that one would only expect to see in a Mediterranean setting.

Whatever the landscape, the monuments, the great cities and the quiet valleys, the real riches of a country are vested in its people. And here Wales is rich indeed. Uniquely talented orators, poets, singers, writers, painters, composers, actors and actresses have been, and continue to be, Wales' gift to the world. The high regard in which the Welsh hold the arts is exemplified in the numerous eisteddfods which are held each year, many of them conducted in the Welsh language and consisting of contests in music and verse. The most famous of these, at Llangollen, now attracts contestants and visitors from all over the world; a virtual Olympics of the arts!

A proud country, Wales. Proud of its language, its traditions, legends and folklore. Proud of its beauty of countryside and shore, certainly. But, above all, proud of its identity and determined to cling to it, whatever the future may bring.

The SMALLEST HOUSE In GREAT BRITAIN

The Smallest House
in Great Britain.

ADMISSION 3ᵈ
NOT OPEN ON SUNDAYS

At any time

Previous page: the tiny house on Conwy Quay, which claims to be the nation's smallest. Left and top: Caerphilly, a Mid-Glamorgan town perhaps more famous for its cheese. Above: the perfectly-concentric castle of Beaumaris on Anglesey, begun in 1295 by Edward I. Facing page: Edward I's massive fortress of Harlech, Gwynedd, begun in 1283. Overleaf: the defences of Pembroke Castle in Dyfed.

Top: 14th-century Carew Castle, Dyfed. Left: the overgrown ruins of Neath Castle, West Glamorgan. Above: Gwrych Castle, near Abergele, Clwyd. Facing page: much restored last century, Castell Coch rises from the trees near Tongwynlais, South Glamorgan. Overleaf: Caerphilly Castle.

Top: a library in Swansea University. Left: the Salon of Erddig, Clwyd, a beautifully-preserved country house. Above: the main building of University College, Cardiff. Facing page, top: the wooden shed at Boat House in Laugharne, Dyfed, where the poet Dylan Thomas worked for 16 years. Facing page, bottom: Plas Newydd, Anglesey, a fine, classic house designed by James Wyatt in 1800. Overleaf: the city of St David's, with its magnificent 12th-century cathedral.

221

Top: the strong walls of Picton Castle, Dyfed, which shelter a fine art collection. Left: the gateway of Beaumaris Castle. Above: the shattered remnants of the Norman keep at Coity Castle, Mid Glamorgan. Facing page: the dining room of Penrhyn Castle, a 19th-century edifice. Overleaf: Cardiff City Hall.

Previous pages: Cardiff Arms Park, home of Welsh rugby. Top and overleaf, right: St David's Cathedral, Dyfed. Left: Talley Abbey, Dyfed. Above and facing page, bottom: founded in 1131, Tintern Abbey, Gwent, was one of the richest monasteries in the region. Facing page, top: Valle Crucis Abbey, near Llangollen. Overleaf: (left) St Asaph Cathedral, Clwyd.

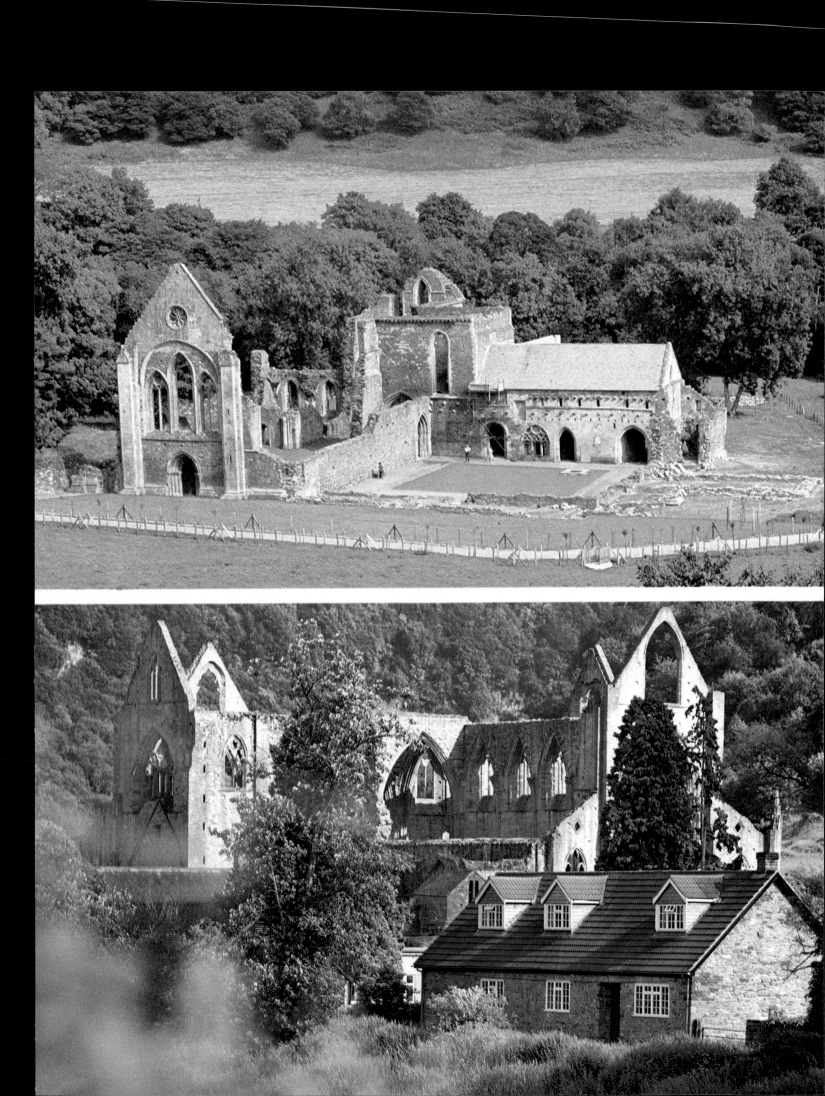

One thousand two hundred years ago most of England came under the sway of King Offa, who built a massive earthwork along his Welsh border. The dyke remains to this day and affords some spectacular views (previous pages) towards Snowdonia. Top: Bird Rock, near Tywyn. Left: the River Dovey at Mallwyd, Gwynedd. Above and facing page: the heights of the Brecon Beacons. Overleaf: Lake Ogwen, Gwynedd.

Previous pages: the Rheidol Valley, Dyfed. Facing page: (top) the Coracle Carnival at Cilgerran, Dyfed, and (bottom) Llyn Gwynant from Hafod Rhisgl, Gwynedd. Top: sheepdog trials at Newbridge-on-Wye, Powys. Right: the Brecon cattle market. Overleaf: the Ogwen Valley, Gwynedd.

Top: one of a series of dams in the Elan Valley of Powys. Left: Llyn Clywedog, a reservoir high above Llandiloes, in Powys. Above: the natural mountain lake of Llyn Padarn, in Gwynedd. Facing page: Llyn Padarn and Llyn Peris from the top of Mount Snowdon. Overleaf: road, rail and river at Ystrad, in the Rhondda.

Top: foxgloves bloom around Solva, a sailing centre on St Brides Bay. Left: the headland and beach at Llangranog, Dyfed. Above: a boat stranded by the tide at Stackpole Quay, Dyfed. Facing page: Llandudno, the largest seaside resort in the principality, stands on Gwynedd's north coast. Its most popular attraction is the huge crescent of beach, backed by a two-mile-long promenade.

Facing page: (top) the Mawddach Estuary and the town of Barmouth, where the National Trust acquired its first property in 1895, and (bottom) Llandudno Pier. Top: Traeth Bychan, on Anglesey. Above: the coast at Rhossili, on the Gower Peninsula. Right: Whitesands Bay, Dyfed. Overleaf: Aberystwyth, Dyfed, where the National Library of Wales preserves many ancient manuscripts as well as modern works.

253

255

Previous pages: Cardiff. Top: South Stack, off
Holy Island, Anglesey. Left: Carreg Ddu,
Gwynedd. Above: Trwyn Yr Wylfa, Gwynedd.
Facing page: Tenby, Dyfed.

The 3,560-foot summit of Snowdon (left) may be reached by footpath (above) or by train (top). Facing page: Snowdon from the west. Overleaf: Gwynedd's Cader Range.

Top: Porthmadog, Gwynedd, whence the Ffestiniog Railway leaves for the mountains. Left: Telford's bridge across the Menai Straits was opened in 1826 and Stephenson's (above) in 1850. Facing page: Portmeirion, Gwynedd, where Sir Clough Williams-Ellis built his dream-like Italianate village.

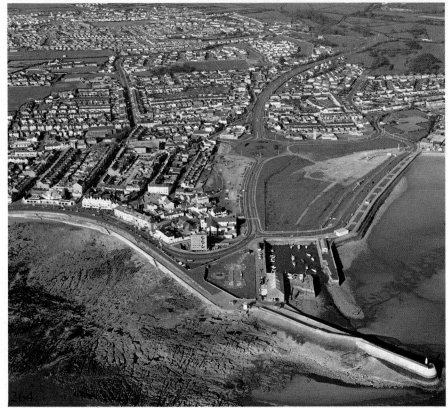

Top: Gwynedd's Mawddach Estuary, with Cader Idris beyond. Left: the South Glamorgan resort of Porthcawl with its tiny Yacht Basin. Above: Telford's Menai Bridge, Facing page: (top) Aberystwyth, Dyfed, and (bottom) Conwy, where the mediaeval walls still encircle the town and the massive castle dominates the scene.
Overleaf: (left) the River Llugwy at Betws-y-Coed and (right) the Aber Falls, near Bangor.

264

Top: the Shropshire Union Canal winds through the hills near Llangollen, with the ruins of the 8th-century castle Dinas Bran atop the hill beyond. Left: the dam at Claerwen. Above: the tranquil waters of the Wye, from the Whitebrook-Redbrook Bridge. Facing page: cattle graze on the slopes above Llangorse Lake, Powys.

Facing page: (top) Tal-y-llyn Lake, Gwynedd, and (bottom) Snowdonia. Top: the River Wye at Longhope Reach, Gwent. Above: a footbridge in Snowdonia National Park. Right: a stream in the North Wales mountains.

SCOTLAND

Scotland is a land of perpetual mystery and enchantment, where the wealth of history and tradition combine with a modern urge and outlook to give an air of magic and excitement unique to the country. A lonely road across the Highlands stretches away over the windswept mountains and the clachans are beacons of warmth and shelter in a desolate landscape. The kingdom is a land where the tide of human emotions has run at its strongest. Claymores and broadswords have been taken to battle by men with revenge in their hearts, and the mists of Glencoe still weep for the MacDonald dead.

But such bloody matters seem a thousand miles from the peaceful Western Isles. Set in a gleaming sea, the dark islands stand like sentinels in the Atlantic. Rising above the long, deep inlets are the heather-covered hills where graze the sheep which produce the wool for the famous Harris tweed. With names like Benbecula and Taransay, the islands are the last bastions of the Gaelic language and culture whose legacy still pervades the Highlands. The small fishing villages lie clustered about the inlets; home to the trawlers that brave the mighty ocean. But the islands are not always so peaceful and calm. During the winter savage storms will sweep the coasts, pounding against the rocks and sending spray high into the wind-wrenched air.

Across the shining Minch, which lies protected behind the wild outer islands, is the almost legendary Isle of Skye. Amidst the scenery of wind-blown heather rise the towers of Dunvegan Castle, where are housed the tattered remains of the Fairy Flag, given to a long dead Macleod of Macleod by his fairy wife. It was to these wild shores and towering mountains that Bonny Prince Charlie came in 1746, after the crushing defeat of his clans at Culloden. After many weeks hiding among the beautiful islands and glens that could never be his, the Prince fled to France, never to return.

As the dark, rolling hills and moors stretch away northwards to the Pentland Firth, the endless vista of bare rock and marshy hollow combine with the howling wind to create an air of wild beauty that cannot be matched anywhere else. The heather-covered hillsides are rich with life. Red deer and grouse are the favourite prey of the hunters who come to these hills during the season. One of the great delights of the Highlands is to tramp for miles across the awe-inspiring landscape, be it in sunshine or in drizzle, and to return to a fireside and a good meal. It is easy to see the magical quality that turns Scottish hearts to the Highlands. Though the bens and glens have seen more than their share of clan feuding and bloodshed, they are now at peace and the great hills are dotted with sheep and trees. But as the gleaming streams wind amongst the heather and the savage wind whips the grass, it is almost as if the plaid-clad men of the past can be seen on their way to wreak vengeance on a neighbouring clan. The majestic scenery of the northern Highlands stretches from Cape Wrath southwards until it is cut short by the Great Glen.

This deep valley slices across the Highlands like a sixty-mile-long sword-cut. The result of great geological forces, this valley runs from Inverness to Fort William and has rightly been called the greatest feature of the Highlands. In its gloomy depths can be found the brooding waters of Loch Ness. Though a great beauty spot and a fine fishing ground, the loch is chiefly known for its monster, hunted in vain by scientists from around the world. On the south side of the glen the land rises again to form the Cairngorm and Grampian Mountains, which are grander than their counterparts on the other side of the Great Glen. These giants are even more impressive when compared to the tiny houses and castles that find shelter beneath the peaks. One of the many homes nestled amid the awesome grandeur is the castle of Balmoral, the favourite Scottish retreat of the Royal Family for well over a century. As well as sheltering the castle of Balmoral, these snowcapped peaks rise above the greatest treasures of Scotland; her distilleries. From these hidden glens and tiny burns the precious amber liquid flows out to all corners of the world, bringing jollity and comradeship to many a lonely heart.

Along the east coast of the Highlands are found the many ports whose fishing fleets set out into the treacherous North Sea in search of herring and mackerel. Aberdeen, Stonehaven and Arbroath may be the largest, but it is Montrose that lives in history. It was James Graham, the Marquess of Montrose, who raised the standard for King Charles in Scotland and won a series of victories against Parliament.

Leaving the dramatic scenery of the desolate Highlands to the north, the rich Lowlands stretch out to the south. Here is found the agricultural wealth of the nation; sheep, cattle and wheat are produced in abundance. The soft beauty of the fertile land is in sharp contrast to the wild grandeur of the mountains and the glens. The rolling agricultural land is suddenly interrupted by the rocky crag at Stirling. Perched on this rocky height, the castle is the centre of the city which lies huddled around its base for protection from the dangers of war. Further down the silvery waters of the Firth of Forth lies the great capital of Scotland; Edinburgh. Standing alone on its rock, the ancient fortress of Edinburgh Castle proudly towers above the city. For centuries it has stood, the centre and focus of history, be it bloody or romantic. The view across the city from the Castle to Palace of Holyroodhouse is truly remarkable, taking in the Royal Mile and the beauties of the 'Athens of the North'. To the west of Edinburgh, on the Clyde, can be found the great industrial heart of the nation. The city of Glasgow spreads out from the river in a mass of business and industrial areas which have made Scotland the nation she is today. But still the heart of every Scot is in the Highlands amid the heather and the tartan.

273

(Previous page) Dunbar Harbour and Castle. (Opposite page) Castle Stalker, ancient home of the Stewarts of Appin, stands on a tiny island off Portnacroish. (This page, top) Loch Arkaig. (Left) amber light warms the scene in rural Strathclyde. (Above) facing Loch Duich, Eilean Donan Castle was bombarded in 1719 by the frigate *Worcester* during a Jacobite rebellion.

275

(Opposite page, top left)
Abbotsford House, Sir Walter
Scott's home in the Borders.
(Remaining pictures) Edinburgh.

277

(This page, top) spanning the Firth of
Forth is the railway bridge, opened in
1890, with the road bridge in the
background and (right) seen from South
Queensferry. (Above) the Palace of
Holyroodhouse, Edinburgh. (Opposite
page, top left) statue of Allan Ramsay
in Princes Street Gardens, Edinburgh.
(Top right) Culzean Castle where, in
1946, Eisenhower was given rooms.
(Bottom) the Forth Road Bridge.

(Opposite page) part of the fishing fleet of Pittenweem. An Augustinian priory was founded here in 1141 and, near the harbour, is the cave-shrine of St Fillan. (This page, far left) sunset over Loch Laggan. (Left) Ben Nevis, the highest mountain in Great Britain at 4,406 ft, seen across the head of Loch Linnhe. (Below) the bay at Morar, famous for its white sands. (Bottom) Loch Katrine's Ellen's Isle features in Sir Walter Scott's *The Lady of the Lake*.

(This page, right) the ruin of Lochranza Castle, which dates from the 16th century, on the Isle of Arran. Its walls overlook Loch Ranza on whose shores, in 1306, Robert the Bruce is believed to have landed from Ireland. He went on to seize the Scottish throne that year, and spent years harrying English forces in his country, eventually defeating them in a set-piece battle at Bannockburn in 1314. He secured English recognition of Scotland's independence by the Treaty of Northampton in 1328. (Below) the sun's rays stream over the peak of Blaven on the Isle of Skye. In the Highland region lies Eilean Donan Castle (opposite page, top) and the crofting and fishing villages of Shieldaig (bottom left) and Plockton (bottom right).

(Opposite page) the River Dochart and (bottom) seen as it flows past Killin. The village overlooks Loch Tay, at the head of which lie the ruins of Finlarig Castle, where can be seen perhaps the only remaining example of an ancient beheading pit. The castle is described in Sir Walter Scott's 1828 novel *The Fair Maid of Perth*. (This page, far left) the hay lies harvested in the fields, ready to be stored when dry for winter feeding, whilst the sheep (left) enjoy the verdant, sun-swept pasture. (Below) springtime at Finstown on the Bay of Firth, Mainland; the largest of over 70 islands in the Orkney group.

(Opposite page and this page, top) the 'Fair City' of Perth, capital of Scotland for a century until 1437, lies at the head of the estuary of the River Tay. (Right) the river seen from Kinnoull Hill. (Above centre) Drummond Castle, near Crieff, was once bombarded by the cannon of Cromwell. (Above) part of the world-famous Gleneagles golf course.

(Opposite page, top) the Caledonian Canal and Ben Nevis and (bottom) the waterway seen at Corpach. The canal (this page, top right and centre left) runs along the Great Glen, connecting several lochs including Loch Linnhe (top left). (Left) Loch Leven and the Glenduror Heights. (Above) the Crinan Canal was built in 1793-1801 so that ships could reach the Atlantic from Loch Fyne, avoiding sailing south.

289

(Opposite page, centre left) Loch Eil; (bottom right) Glen Orchy. (Remaining pictures) Glencoe, which means the 'glen of weeping' in Gaelic, was the scene of the treacherous attack upon the Macdonalds by men under the control of Archibald Campbell, the 10th Earl of Argyll. When King James II was replaced on the throne by William of Orange in 1689, many clans stayed loyal to James. So, in August 1691, the government offered indemnity to all chiefs who swore allegiance before 1st January, 1692. The chiefs accepted, but brave Alexander Macdonald decided to leave his oath-taking until 31st December, 1691, the day before the deadline. When it was discovered that there was no magistrate in Fort William to take his oath, it was delayed until the 6th. By way of dire example, 100 soldiers made welcome by the Macdonalds for over a week, suddenly attacked their hosts on 13th February; 38 were slaughtered, including the chief; others died later in the snow.

(These pages) Edinburgh. (Above) the Scott Monument in Princes Street Gardens. Pipers (below and opposite page) and (right) at the Military Tatoo. (Bottom right) memorial to the Royal Scots Greys.

(This page, top) Loch Ard lies within the Queen Elizabeth Forest Park. (Right) Loch Affric, near Cannich. (Below) Loch Awe and Kilchurn Castle, held by Lord Breadalbane during the '45 to prevent the Jacobites marching south by this route. (Opposite page, top left) Glen Clova and the Grampians. (Top right) the Lochan Fada. (Bottom) the River Leny at Callander, north of Stirling.

(Opposite page and this page, bottom right) the harbour of Pittenweem. (Left) the luxury liner *Queen Elizabeth II* sails past Cloch Point, in the outer reaches of the Clyde estuary, where stands a lighthouse built in 1797. Facing it stands the resort of Dunoon. The ship, used to carry soldiers during the Falklands Campaign, was built on Clydeside and launched in September 1967. (Below) Easdale. (Bottom left) Anstruther.

(This page, top) Loch Moy. Nearby,
the 'Rout of Moy' took place
during the '45, when men under
Lord Loudoun's command fled in
disarray. (Above) Loch Garry.
(Right) Loch Ness, whose monster
was first seen by St Columba in AD
565. (Opposite page, top) Loch
Eil. (Bottom) Loch Tummel.

(This page, top) the lighthouse at Cantick Head. (Right) Badcall. (Below) the Stacks of Duncansby lie off the coast near John O' Groats (opposite page, top). (Bottom left) Blair Castle is said to have been the last in Britain to withstand siege. (Bottom right) Dunbeath Castle.

(This page, right) Loch Ainort on the Isle of Skye. (Far right) Urquhart Castle, overlooking Loch Ness, raised by the Lords of the Isles, was sacked by Edward I. Robert the Bruce lay siege to and held the castle. It was blown up in 1692 to prevent its occupation by Jacobites. (Below) Loch Tummel seen from Queen's View. (Bottom left) Loch Eilt, which is bordered by the famous Road to the Isles. (Bottom right) Castle Stalker, which dates from about 1500, is associated with James IV, and the Royal Coat of Arms is carved over the entrance. (Opposite page) Loch Creran.

(These pages) Aberdeen, an important university and maritime city, lies on the estuaries of the Rivers Dee and Don. The charters for the city date back to about 1179. Edward I came to Aberdeen in 1296 and, after a battle in Methven Wood in 1306, Robert the Bruce did too. The city's motto, *Bon Accord*, was the rallying cry of the Bruces. Edward III burnt the city in 1337 and Montrose occupied the city three times. Today, the Municipal Buildings incorporate the Old Tolbooth, scene of public executions until 1857, which preserves the 'Aberdeen Maiden' – the instrument on which the French guillotine was modelled.

(This page, top) the magnificent, rugged peaks of the Cuillins of Skye. (Above) Stromness, Orkney Islands, looks across Hoy Sound and southeast to Scapa Flow, the former base of the Grand Fleet. (Right) Strath Mashie. (Opposite page, top) Lerwick, Shetland Islands. King Haco of Norway came to the harbour in 1263, before the Battle of Largs. (Bottom) Skara Brae, Mainland, in the Orkney Islands, is a Stone Age village still remaining in a good state of preservation.

(Opposite page and this page, centre left) Mallaig Harbour lies on North Morar, the last point on the Road to the Isles: 'By Ailort and Morar to the sea'. (Above centre) the Crinan Canal allows vessels from the Clyde to avoid making the long and sometimes stormy rounding of the Mull of Kintyre. (Top) Ayr Harbour. (Above) the Caledonian Canal, begun in 1803 by Thomas Telford, took 44 years to complete. (Left) the ruins of Castle Moil stand to the east of Kyleakin, Isle of Skye.

(These pages) Scotland, land of the claymore, clansmen warriors and castle keeps. (Right) Castle Stalker and (above and opposite page, top right) Eilean Donan Castle. (Left) Inverlochy Castle by Ben Nevis. (Bottom right) next to Loch Awe lies Kilchurn Castle, built in 1440, of which Wordsworth wrote, 'Child of loud-throated War! the mountain-stream roars in thy hearing; but thy hour of rest is come, and thou art silent in thy age'.

(Opposite page, top) haunted, 17th-century Glamis Castle, where the Old Pretender sojourned in 1715. (Centre left) Stirling Castle, recaptured from the English by Wallace in 1297, it was lost again in 1304 following a siege by Edward I. General Monk succeeded in taking the castle in 1651, but Prince Charles Edward failed in 1746. (Centre right) Urquhart Castle stands above Loch Ness. (Bottom left) Inverary Castle, on the shores of Loch Fyne, is the seat of the Duke of Argyll, head of Clan Campbell. (Bottom right) Balmoral Castle, the Queen's Highland home. (This page, top) the keep of Kilchurn Castle at Loch Awe was built in 1440 by Sir Colin Campbell, founder of the family of Breadalbane. (Left) the castle of Eilean Donan, whose name commemorates Saint Donan of Eigg, murdered by Norsemen.

(Opposite page) Balmoral Castle, rebuilt by the Prince Consort in the Scottish Baronial style, was first mentioned in 1484 when it was known as Bouchmorale. (This page, left) ruined Elgin Cathedral dates from the 13th century. (Above) Crathes Castle, north of the River Dee. (Bottom left) Loch Faskally, created by the dam at Pitlochry. At Balquhidder, not far from Loch Voil (bottom right) is the burial place of Robert MacGregor, 'Rob Roy', who died in 1734. He was a freebooter who managed to live a life of plunder and then receive a pardon in 1727. (Below right) Blair Castle, ancient seat of Clan Murray.

315

(This page) St Andrews. (Far right) the square, 108-foot-high tower of the early-12th century St Rule's Church, now a ruin. In the cemetery nearby is buried Tom Morris (1821-1908), the famous golfer. (Right) the famous Road Hole, the Seventeenth, on the Old Course of The Royal and Ancient Golf Club of St Andrews (opposite page, top left), founded in 1754. (Bottom left) the cathedral in St Andrews was founded in 1160. King James V and Mary of Guise were married here and, in 1559, John Knox gave sermons within its walls. (Top right and bottom right) Crail and its harbour. (Centre right) St Monance.

(Opposite page, bottom) Loch Morlich and the Cairngorms. Glenmore Lodge, the well-known mountaineering training centre, can be found here. (Top and this page, above) the ski centre of Aviemore. (Top) Glenfinnan Viaduct, situated above Loch Shiel. (Centre left) Loch Etive is a sea loch which extends from the Firth of Lorne to the foot of Glen Etive. (Far left) snow covers the banks of Loch Leven. (Left) Ben Nevis seen from the Highland village of Tulloch.

(This page, top left) the Bullers of Buchan is a 200-foot-deep chasm in the cliffs two miles northeast of Cruden Bay. (Top right) Scalloway lies west of Lerwick in the Shetland Islands. Nearby is Gallows Hill, where witches used to be burnt. (Centre right) a ship calls at Mid Yell, also in the Shetlands. (Above) sunset silhouettes Skye's Cuillin mountain ridge. (Right) the peak of Blaven which, at 3,042 feet, overlooks beautiful Loch na Creitheach. (Opposite page) St Margaret's Hope, on the northern coast of South Ronaldsay in the Orkney Islands, is linked by its name to Queen Margaret, the 'Maid of Norway', who died in 1290 on board a ship bound for Scotland.

(Opposite page, top left and this page, left) the Isle of Mull. Dr Johnson visited the island in 1773 but his comment was, 'O Sir! a most dolorous country'. (Above, top and opposite page, top right) Oban Harbour is dominated by the large, circular stone structure known as McCaig's Folly. In the town, Dr Johnson and Boswell found themselves a 'tolerable' inn. (Bottom) the village of Findochty, between Long Head and Craig Head.

(Opposite page) Ben Nevis seen across the head of Loch Linnhe with Fort William on the far shore. (This page, far left) the twin Buchaille Etive peaks above the climbers' hut. (Left) a fine example of Highland cattle. (Below) Ben Nevis seen from Banavie. (Bottom left) erected in 1815 by Macdonald of Glenaladale, this monument commemorates Charles Edward Stuart's meeting with Lochiel and faithful supporters on 18th August, 1745. (Bottom right) the bagpipe's wail, sweet music of freedom echoing in the Highlands.

(Opposite page, top) Dundee seen from Newport-on-Tay with the Tay Road Bridge (centre left and right), completed in 1966, spanning the river's girth.
(Bottom left) spring flowers beside a burn in Aberfeldy. Here can be found the Black Watch Monument, erected in 1887 – Queen Victoria's Jubilee Year – to commemorate the founding of the regiment 150 years earlier.
(Bottom right) some 15 miles to the west of Perth lies the village of Crieff. Charles Edward Stuart, in 1746, held a council of war here in the 'Drummond Arms'. A few miles away is Drummond Castle.
(This page, left) the Tay Road Bridge and (below) crossing the Firth of Tay are the new road bridge and the two-mile-long Tay Railway Bridge of 1887.

(This page, right) Loch Ness, famous for its monster, which can hide away in an estimated 263,000,000,000 cubic feet of water. (Below) near Spean Bridge is the bronze Commando Memorial, designed by Scott Sutherland in 1952, which commemorates those who trained here during World War II. (Bottom left) Loch Eil. (Bottom right) Castle Stalker. (Opposite page) Whiteness Voe.

(This page, top and right) Glasgow and the River Clyde. (Below) the Cross of Lorraine on Lyle Hill, Greenock, overlooking the Firth of Clyde, is a monument to Free French sailors who died in the Battle of the Atlantic. (Bottom right) the beautiful bay at Oban. (Opposite page, top) wharves beyond the River Clyde's Kingston Bridge. (Bottom left) Glasgow's 19th-century University Buildings with the City Chambers on George Square (bottom right).

(Opposite page, bottom) Dumfries on the banks of the River Nith, which is crossed by the 15th-century Old Bridge, used only as a footbridge today. Interesting places in the town include the Burns House, where Robert Burns died in 1796. On a building in Castle Street there is a plaque marking the place where, in 1306, Robert Bruce is said to have stabbed the 'Red Comyn' in the former Greyfriars monastery church. (Top) the Burns Monument seen from the Brig O'Doon, Alloway, and the statue (this page, below) are Ayr's tribute to the famous Scottish poet. (Far left) Kilchurn Castle, used as a garrison for Hanoverian soldiers in 1746. (Left) Blair Castle, Blair Atholl. The seat of the Duke of Atholl, head of Clan Murray, he has the rare privilege of being a British subject who is allowed to have his own private army; the Atholl Highlanders.

(This page, above) Port of
Menteith. (Right) Loch Garten. The
schooner *Captain Scott* (below) on
Loch Eil (below right). (Bottom)
Largs where, in 1263, King Haco of
Norway was defeated in battle.
(Opposite page) the Glenduror
Heights across Loch Leven.

IRELAND

The last outpost of Europe before the rolling swell of the mighty Atlantic, Ireland is a land with a glorious landscape; a landscape shaped by the people who have lived there and by their way of life. But above all Ireland is a land shaped by the Celts. From the time that they first arrived, with their fiery tempers and artistic imagination, they have shaped the land to themselves. The constant warfare of the Irish chieftains and kings has left its mark in the ring forts and ruined towers dotting the scenery; buildings that recall the great heyday of Irish culture when chiefs led their warriors into battle and held court in huge halls to the sound of bardic harps.

Today, the Gaelic tradition is strongest in the west where the traditional rural life has been least disturbed. Here, too, the savage grandeur of the Atlantic coast is at its best. Throughout the long winter, storms lash the Connemara coast, throwing spray into the air and ringing the dark hills with a line of shining light. The great rollers that mercilessly pound the headlands and bays have been swept across the breadth of the ocean and release the pent-up energies of a thousand miles upon the wild shores of Galway. But in the summer, when gentle waves lap the shoreline, the treacherous rocks take on an air of limitless romance and enchantment. To the south of Connemara lies perhaps the most famous part of the Irish coast, Galway Bay. When the waters of the deep, broad inlet glitter in the evening sunlight and the sea birds wheel across the sky it is easy to see why this stretch of water has inspired the poetic genius of the Irish for generations.

Further south the Shannon spills into the ocean between Loop and Kerry Heads after a sluggish journey of some two hundred miles, fifty of which are along the tidal estuary. Beyond the Shannon Estuary the already scenic coast becomes truly spectacular as long fingers of rock push out into the blue ocean. The long inlets along this section of the coast are, in reality, sunken river valleys and the drowned contours can still be glimpsed. Perhaps the most beautiful of all these submerged valleys is Dingle Bay. The rich, verdant fields stretch across the land right to the edge of the cliffs that plunge down to the blue waters. Small, sandy bays are dominated by the rising mountains of County Kerry in the distance. Another of the bays, Bantry Bay, is famed far and wide as a deep water anchorage and can handle the largest oil tankers.

East of Kerry and its wild coastline lies the county of Cork. The southern coast shares much of the dramatic grandeur of the Atlantic coast, but is chiefly made up of charming bays beloved by holiday-makers. Off shore lies a string of islands famous for their wildlife and charm. Despite its more tranquil, peaceful air, this coast has seen its fair share of maritime disasters. In 1979, a yacht race from England around the Fastnet Rock ended in disaster when an unexpected storm sank many ships, and in 1917 the *Lusitania* was torpedoed off the Old Head of Kinsale. Upriver from Cobh, in the valley of the Lee, is the far-famed Blarney Castle. This great stronghold was built by McCarthy Laidir, who was descended from the kings of Munster, but it is not for its history that Blarney is known. Set high up in the wall of the keep, just below the battlements, is the Blarney Stone. It is rumoured that to kiss this stone bestows the 'gift-of-the-gab'.

The great scenic beauty of the west shoreline of Ireland is due to the strength of the rocks along its coast. It is these same rocks that form the beautiful, windswept mountains of Connaught and Munster. Stretching back from the coast are the uplands of the 'barren west'. The thin soils of the hills make them suitable for little except grazing and tourism. The hordes of visitors who come to the region in the summer for the scenery and the fishing bring an excitement and vitality to the area that has been lacking for centuries. In the Macgillicuddy's Reeks of Munster is the tallest mountain in Ireland, Carrantuohill, some three and a half thousand feet high. This line of high ground extends around most of the coast of Ireland giving a fine backdrop to the lovely coastal scenery.

Inland from the ring of mountains is a broad, undulating plateau of fertile land. It is here that the scenery reaches the typical view of the Emerald Isle and there are truly forty shades of green. Small crofts nestle amid the lush landscape where cattle and sheep are grazed and crops grown in abundance. It is as if the area is determined to make all the idealised pictures of Ireland come true. It is not only the soils and contours of the plateau that have created the landscape but the climate. Ireland's mild, wet climate is ideal for the crops and livestock that are so much a part of the scenery of the 'typical Ireland'.

Unlike the turbulent streams of the coastal mountains the rivers of the plateau are slow and sluggish, often becoming lakes or bogs along their courses. The Shannon flows from the slopes of Tiltinbane, County Cavan, through the whole of the central plateau to meet the sea at Limerick. Along its gentle path it flows through some of the loveliest land in Ireland and forms Loughs Derg and Ree. Loughs and bogs are among the great features of Irish landscape, spread across the face of the land. The bogs have their own part to play in the life of the nation. The peat they yield continues to be an important source of fuel for both home and industry.

From the mountains of Donegal to the valley of the Lee, Ireland is a truly beautiful country of green. Here the mind can drift back to days long gone; a time when life moved at a slower pace enfolded in the beauty of nature.

(Opposite page) Melmore Head, Rosguill Peninsula, County Donegal. (This page, top left) Achill Island, the largest island off the Irish coast, in County Mayo. (Top right) Slea Head, Dingle Peninsula, County Kerry. (Above) Waterlily Bay, Lough Currane. (Centre right) near Killarney, County Kerry. (Right) the view across Lough Corrib, near Cornamona, County Galway.

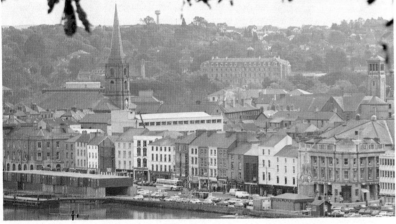

(This page, above) the city of Waterford, first settled by Norsemen in the mid-9th century. Reginald, son of Sigtryg, is reputed to have built the first church here, about 1050, where Christ Church now stands. The town's loyalty to the throne was demonstrated when the pretenders, Lambert Simnel and Perkin Warbeck, were refused admission. The latter, with the Earl of Desmond, laid siege to Waterford for twelve days without success. In reward, the city was given the right to the device *Intacta manet Waterfordia*. In 1649, it managed to repulse Cromwell's siege, too. (Top left and opposite page) stages in the making of world-famous Waterford crystal. (This page, top right) Muckross House, Killarney, County Kerry, where the skills of traditional weaving (centre right and right) may be seen.

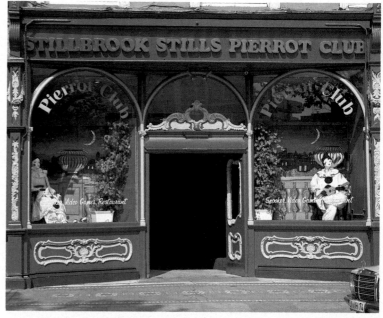

(Opposite page) colourful shopfronts line the streets of Dublin. (This page) the shoe department (left), food hall (above left and above right) and saddlery (top right) in Brown Thomas's on Grafton Street. (Top left and centre left) Greene's Bookshop on Clare Street. Dublin was known to Ptolemy who, in AD 140, marked it on a map as Eblana. Later, it was known as *Baile Átha Cliath*, the Town of the Hurdle Ford, by which it is known in Gaelic today. The site of the ford in its name is today spanned by Father Mathew Bridge. The blackish-looking waters of the Liffey as they reach the sea are responsible for the name of Dublin, for *Dubh Linn* means 'Dark Pool'. It was the Danes who developed the city as they found it a useful base for operations. Good Friday, 1014, saw their power destroyed by Brian Boru and his fierce Irish warriors at the Battle of Clontarf.

(These pages) in the pubs and clubs of Ireland is found the essential Irish love of song, laughter and a drink at the end of a hard working day. One of the popular kinds of drinking establishment is the singing pub, such as Hough's Pub (far left) in Banagher, County Offaly. The customers do the singing as they imbibe the traditional drinks of whiskey and stout. Irish whiskey, spelt correctly with an 'e', has a distinctive flavour not to be confused with Scotch whisky. The most famous stout in Ireland comes from the Dublin brewery in St James's Gate – Guinness – though it no longer arrives at pubs in wooden barrels but in metal kegs known affectionately as 'iron lungs'.

(These pages) the National Gallery of Ireland stands on the north side of Leinster Lawn. The building was designed by Francis Fowke and was opened in 1864. Housed within the same building is the National Portrait Gallery. The art gallery was originally financed by public subscription and, today, also receives one-third of the royalties accruing to the estate of George Bernard Shaw, whose statue (above left) by Paul Troubetzkoy stands by the entrance. Although there are naturally many examples from the Irish School, it is well known for its Dutch masters – including Rembrandt's *Rest on the Flight into Egypt* – and works of 17th-century Italian, French and Spanish Schools. There is also English work by Gainsborough and Hogarth. Work by Irish artists include landscapes by Nathaniel Hone and important portraits by John Butler Yeats. Several fine sculptures are displayed, too.

(Opposite page) Ballycopeland Windmill, County Down. (This page, left) St Patrick at Croagh Patrick, County Mayo, and notice to pilgrims (above). (Bottom left) Calvary statue, Healy Pass. (Below) Christ the King and Glen of Aherlow.

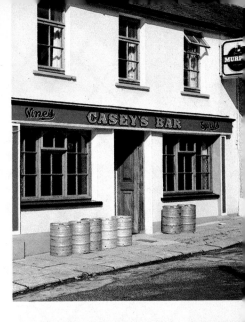

AR AN LÁĊAIR SEO DO ŠEAS
AN ĊIŠ INAR RUŠAD
DIARMAID Ó DONNABÁIN ROSA
·FÍNÍN AŠUS TÍRŠRÁĊÓIR·
·1831 - 1915·
On this site stood the house
wherein was born
Jeremiah O'Donovan Rossa
Fenian and Patriot
That brave and splendid Gael
unconquered and unconquerable

"NÍ DÉANFAID ŠAEL DEARMAD
ORC ŠO DRÁĊ NA DREIĊE"

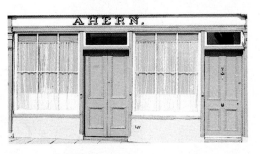

Far left: a variety of boats moored at
Kinsale, Co Cork. The town features
prominently in Irish history.
Remaining pictures: brightly-painted
shops and pubs in Cork and (above
centre), a plaque commemorating
O'Donovan Rossa.

(Opposite page) Kilkenny Castle. (This page, top) the Rock of Cashel. Here, in the 5th century, the King of Munster erected a *cashel* or stone fort. St Patrick preached there on the subject of the Trinity, explaining its nature by using the trefoil shamrock. The 13th-century cathedral was burnt in 1495 by Gerald, Earl of Kildare. He told Henry VII that he did it because he thought the Archbishop was inside! (Left) Galway's Salmon Weir Bridge. (Above) Dunguaire Castle, Kinvarra, County Galway.

(Opposite page) Adare Manor, County
Limerick, was the seat of the Earl of
Dunraven. (This page, left) Headford House.
the magnificent estate of the Marquess of
Headford. (Top) Bangor Castle, County Down,
is an imitation English manor house which
was built in the 1850s. (Below) Castletown
House, County Kildare, is one of the finest
Georgian houses in Ireland, and the
headquarters of the Irish Georgian Society.

(This page, top left) near Partry, County Mayo, stands Ballintubber Abbey, known as the 'Abbey which Refused to Die'. Founded by Cathal O'Conor, King of Connaught, for Austin canons in 1216, it has been in continuous use for over 750 years. It had to be largely rebuilt after it was swept by fire in 1270 and has recently been renovated. (Above) Dunluce Castle, County Antrim, lies three miles from Portrush. The site has revealed evidence of early Christian and Viking occupation. In 1588, guns from the Spanish Armada ship *Gerona*, wrecked on nearby rocks, were used by Sorley Boy MacDonnell to reinforce the castle's defences. (Bottom left) close to the Rock of Cashel, County Tipperary, is Hore Abbey which was built by the Cistercians. (Left, below right and opposite page) Clonmacnoise, County Offaly. *Cluain Mhic Nóis*, The Meadow of the Son of Nós, is where a monastery was founded in AD 547 by St Ciarán. He had been given the land by Diarmaid Mac Cerbhaill of the royal house of the Uí Néill, who helped him to build the first wooden church there and became High King soon afterwards. There are extensive remains here today including O'Rourke's Tower (opposite page), dating from AD 1124, and the 12th-century church of St Finghin (this page, below right) with its round tower.

(These pages) Dublin still retains fine examples of colourful, elegant Georgian architecture. Today, some of the best Georgian mansions may be seen lining Merrion Square, St Stephen's Green and in the neighbouring streets. Important Georgian houses include Leinster House (1745), which is the work of designer Richard Cassels who also designed Newman House on St Stephen's Green. Leinster House, originally known as Kildare House, is now the seat of the *Dáil Éireann* (the House of Representatives) and the *Seanad Éireann* (the Senate).

(Opposite page) Dunbrody Abbey, County Wexford, was built about 1182. Because its charter gave the right of sanctuary, it also became known as St Mary of Refuge. (This page, above and top left) the Augustinian Abbey at Cong, County Mayo, was founded by Roderick O'Connor, the last King of Ireland. (Top right) the restored Cistercian Abbey at Holycross, County Tipperary, founded in 1169. (Centre right) Cahir Castle, County Tipperary. (Right) the Rock of Cashel, ancient seat of the kings of Munster. In the 18th century, the lead was taken off the Cathedral roof and sold by Archbishop Price.

(Left) University College, Cork, is situated on Western Road, to the west of St Fin Barre's Cathedral. It was founded in 1845 under the name of Queen's College, Victoria being the Queen in question. The fine building is made from carboniferous limestone and was erected on the site of 7th-century Gill Abbey. The library's collection includes some Ogham stones, Ogham being the early form of Irish writing. There are also several early, locally-printed books. In the grounds is the Honan Collegiate Chapel of 1915 with stained-glass windows by Harry Clarke and Sarah Purser. (Top and above) Ashford Castle, County Galway, is half a mile southwest of Cong, over the border in County Mayo. Built originally on the shores of Lough Corrib by the Oranmore and Browne family as a shooting lodge in the 18th century, it was later the home of Sir Benjamin Lee Guinness. He much improved the land and added to the size of the estate. On the western side of the castle may be seen the coat of arms of one of the members of the Guinness family; Lord Ardilaun. The property was bought in 1939 to become a luxury hotel.

(These pages) Ireland: land of sweeping hillsides dotted with sheep, tiny villages, quiet country lanes and a sense of peace which goes with a more leisurely pace of life. (Above) going to Belmullet's market, County Mayo. (Below) dry-stone walls march over the fields where the horse has not been supplanted.

(These pages) scenes in rural Ireland; spanning the rhythm of the seasons in a cycle that reaches back through the millennia. (Below) the scythe sweeps whispering through the tall grass and lays the swaths softly in sweet-smelling rows. (Bottom left) on the Muckross Estate, Killarney, County Kerry, may be seen a folk museum where the blacksmith shows his skill.

(Opposite page) Glenoe, from the Gaelic *Gleann Eo* meaning Yew Valley, is found in County Antrim. (This page, top left and left) the Sheeffry Hills near Delphi, County Mayo. (Top right) travelling in a jaunting car. (Above) a day out rock-climbing. (Centre left) young child and donkey, faithful friends in this land which lies wrapped in time's mist-laden kingdom, held golden in the hearts and memories of those that have left its shores, a country of verdant green; beloved Ireland.

(Opposite page) Tollymore Forest Park, County Down. (This page, above) near Moll's Gap, County Kerry, and the Owenreagh River (left). (Below) Lough Key Forest Park.

Storm gives way to sun, and rainbows – Nature's kaleidoscopic brushwork – sweep across the sky. (Left) St Mary's Cathedral, Killarney, County Kerry, is a Gothic-Revival church dating from 1842-1855 and designed by A.W. Pugin. It was renovated in the early 1970s at a cost of £278,500 when damaged plasterwork was removed to reveal the natural stone beneath. (Above) Father Mathew Memorial Church (1832) and Parliament Bridge (1806) in Cork. The church, with its soaring, graceful lantern spire, was designed by George Richard Pain and was the church of the Capuchin convent where Father Theobald Mathew – the 'apostle of Temperance' – was the Superior.

(These pages) land of raging torrents, foaming cataracts, and bournes the colour of whiskey as they flow over the rocks beneath. As the sun's light touches the river's relentless downward path (top left) it freezes for a moment in time the maelstrom of the waters. (Opposite page) the Owenriff River. (This page, top left) cascades on the Owenreagh River below Moll's Gap, County Kerry. (Top right) Aasleagh Falls, near Leenane, County Galway. (Above) Glencar Lake, County Leitrim. (Right) Ballynahinch, County Galway.

(Opposite page and this page, above) Mount Usher Gardens planted by the Walpole family. (Top and right) the Japanese Gardens at Tully House, Kildare. Lord Wavertree employed forty gardeners from Japan to produce this masterpiece. Wending through the gardens is the 'Path of Life', symbolic of man and the stages of his time on earth.

(Opposite page and this page, far left) the Dublin Spring Show. (Remaining pictures) an exciting day out at the Galway Races.

(These pages) Dublin Castle. (This page, far left) the main staircase in the State Apartments. (Left) the Portrait Gallery. (Below) the Drawing Room of the State Apartments with its magnificent chandeliers. The castle has been much altered since it was first commenced in 1204 by Myler FitzHenry, grandson of Henry I. The main entrance is at Cork Hill where, on the old main gate, the heads of Irish chieftains who defied English rule were displayed on spikes. The Bermingham Tower, which dates from 1411, used to be the State Prison and from it, in the 16th century, Red Hugh O'Donnell managed to escape to lead revolt against the English forces. In 1534, the castle withstood siege by Thomas Fitzgerald. It was the official seat of the lords lieutenant until the Free State of 1922.

(These pages) the Irish have always been close to the sea in spirit. (Opposite page) Dunmore East is an angling resort at the mouth of Waterford Harbour. (This page, top left) Kinsale, County Cork, was occupied by the Spanish under the command of Don Juan d'Aguila in 1601 but Mountjoy forced them to surrender. (Above) Killybegs, a busy fishing port in County Donegal. (Left) fishing in County Galway. (Right) the *Saint Jude*, at Carna, County Galway.

(This page, below) in Kenmare, County Kerry, salmon hang racked ready to be smoked to satisfy the gourmet's palate. The town was founded in 1670 by Sir William Petty (1623-1687) and colonized by about 75 Englishmen. They managed to establish a fishery and ironworks but were regularly under attack. In 1688, they were assaulted by 3,000 men and had to flee in two vessels, 'packed like fish one upon the other'. They reached Bristol after a fortnight. (Remaining pictures) Killybegs has a fine harbour on a small inlet of Donegal Bay.

(Opposite page) the Grand Canal, to the south of the River Liffey. (This page, top left and left) Phoenix Park, Dublin. (Above) thatched cottage on the Kenmare Estate, Killarney, County Kerry. Leisure time spent angling (below left) and horse riding (below).

388

(Opposite page) St Patrick's Cathedral, Dublin, on the site of the Holy Well where the saint baptized converts. (This page, top) Franciscan Friary in County Wexford. (Above left) church interior in Cork. (Above right) inside the Church of Christ the King, Cork. (Right) stained-glass window in St Canice's Cathedral, Kilkenny.

(Opposite page and this page, top left) the National Museum, Dublin, houses some of the best examples of early Christian art to be found in Europe. Here may be seen the Feakle Treasure, found in 1948 in County Clare; many Bronze Age gold ornaments; the Ardagh Chalice, and the Cross of Cong which once held a fragment of the True Cross. (Far left and left) the 'Long Room' of Trinity College, Dublin. The flat plaster ceiling was replaced by the present barrel-shaped ceiling in 1856-1862. (Top and above) exhibits within the Rothgory Transport Museum in Dunleer, County Louth.

The hospitality to be found in the Emerald Isle is legendary. A warm welcome is assured to all who come to sample the fayre offered by the country's restaurants and hotels and the delectable delights contained within to please the tourist's tastes. (Opposite page) The King Sitric is one of Ireland's most attractive and successful seafood restaurants, being highly rated in the *Good Food Guide to Ireland.* (This page, left, far left and centre left) 'The English Market' in Cork. (Below, bottom left and bottom right) colourful Dublin Market and the shoppers who frequent its stalls.

393

(Opposite page) sunset over Glenbeigh on the Ring of Kerry. (Left) Clifden Bay, Connemara. (Above) view over Kingstown Bay from Sky Road, west of Clifden, County Galway. (Below) stormy sky at Slyne Head.

(Opposite page and this page, left) passing through the heart of Dublin is the River Liffey, stained a myriad shades of colour by setting sun or city lights. (Below) Bangor, County Down, is a famous seaside resort. St Comgall was born nearby, close to Black Head, and he founded his missionary abbey at Bangor about AD 555. He attracted many pupils and at one time had over 3,000 students. From these shores his evangelising disciples would set forth to preach the Gospel to the heathen Germanic tribes of central Europe. St Gall and St Columbanus were among those who went to convert them. Eventually, the fame of the monastery attracted the scourge of the land – the Norsemen – who destroyed all with fire and sword in AD 824. Several thousand died in that raid. About 1140, Abbot Malachy rebuilt the abbey. The Normans gave it to the Augustinians but the abbey was dissolved in 1542.

(Opposite page) donkeys on the Cooley
Peninsula, County Louth. (This page, top
left) collecting peat for the hearth. (Top
right) man, and his friends through ages
past: dog and patient horse. (Centre right)
in County Galway. Indoor cattle market
(left) in County Donegal (above). (Overleaf)
the Mourne Mountains, County Down.